LITTLE MONSTER'S
WORD BOOK

To Justine McNair

BY MERCER MAYER

inchworm
PRESS
TM

A MERCER MAYER LTD. / J.R. SANSEVERE BOOK

MERCER MAYER'S LITTLE MONSTER WORD BOOK book, characters, text and images © 1977, 1998 Mercer Mayer.
Previously published in a different format by Golden Press.
LITTLE MONSTER is a registered trademark of Orchard House Licensing Company.
MERCER MAYER'S LITTLE MONSTER and MERCER MAYER'S LITTLE MONSTER LOGO are trademarks of Orchard House Licensing Company.

Letters

A ngry anchovy

B ig bite

C up of cola

D own the drain

E at everything

F etch the fiddle

G ive a grin

H old him

I t is icky

J umping jack-in-the-box

K icking kerploppus

L eaping lizards

M uch mud

Not nice

Open oyster

Paint the pail

Quilt a quilt

Rubber raft

Smelly shoe

Trollusk tears

Usually unlucky

Very vain vampire

Wash the walrus

X-ray

Your yellow yarn

Zipperump-a-zoo

Dress-up

Birthday Party

balloons

paper lanterns

egg-and-spoon race

cup

egg

punch bowl

sack race

camera

blindfold

party hat

candles

birthday boy

birthday cake

pin the tail

party favor

bowl

fork

plate

tablecloth

presents

ice cream and cake

hot dog

tree house

bird

butterfly

lean-to

barbecue

flashlight

CAMPING

camper

canteen

sleeping bag

tent

cattails

ants

picnic basket

rowboat

radio

oar

PICNIC

lily pad

cold milk

thermos

picnic table

Summertime

kite

HAY RIDE

kite
string

somersaults

fishing
pole

can
of worms

bathing
cap

FISHING

bathing
suit

WATERSKIING

water skis

sail

mast

pond

SWIMMING

BOATING

sailboat

snow castle

ski lift

snow shovel

SLEDDING

sled

top hat

sticks

SNOWBALL FIGHT

gloves

snow

jacket

snowballs

ice fangs

thermos

hot chocolate

ice skate

BUILDING A SNOW MONSTER

ICE SKATING

Wintertime

SLEIGH RIDE

ski poles

ski boots

skis

SKIING

ICE HOCKEY

hockey stick

mittens

hole

line

fish

ICE FISHING

puck

mast

earmuffs

sail

scarf

boots

ICE BOATING

runner

Holidays

HALLOWEEN

witch

fake nose

candy bags

devil

skeleton

jack-o'-lantern

VALENTINE'S DAY

hearts

red paper

paste

paper lace

scissors

EASTER

Easter bunny suit

dyeing eggs

yellow

red

purple

THANKSGIVING

roast turkey

pumpkin pie

Pilgrim

Pilgrim

turkey

jelly beans

Easter basket

chocolate bunny

SAINT PATRICK'S DAY

four leaf clover

FOURTH OF JULY

American flag

Roman candle

rocket

firecracker

sparklers

star

Christmas tree

ball

candy cane

Santa Claus

Nativity scene

Three Wise Men

stockings

fireplace

CHRISTMAS

pajamas

gingerbread critters

milk

holly

stand

presents

Carnival

roller coaster

barn

silo

BUMPER CARS

prize tomato

farmer

tractor

cow

goat

sheep

horse

DONKEY
AND
CTURE TAKEN

SHOOTING GALLERY

HIT THE BOTTLE

teddy bears

pinwheels

milk bottles

cotton candy

camera

photographer

Things to Be When You Get Bigger

farmer

truck driver

fire fighter

police officer

doctor

gas station attendant

baker

storekeeper

astronaut

mail carrier

scuba diver

photographer

artist

author

telephone operator

librarian

dentist

cabinetmaker

florist

bird watcher

general

veterinarian

sailor

pilot

animal trainer

waiter

magician

juggler

taxi driver

actor

actress

hobo

Numbers

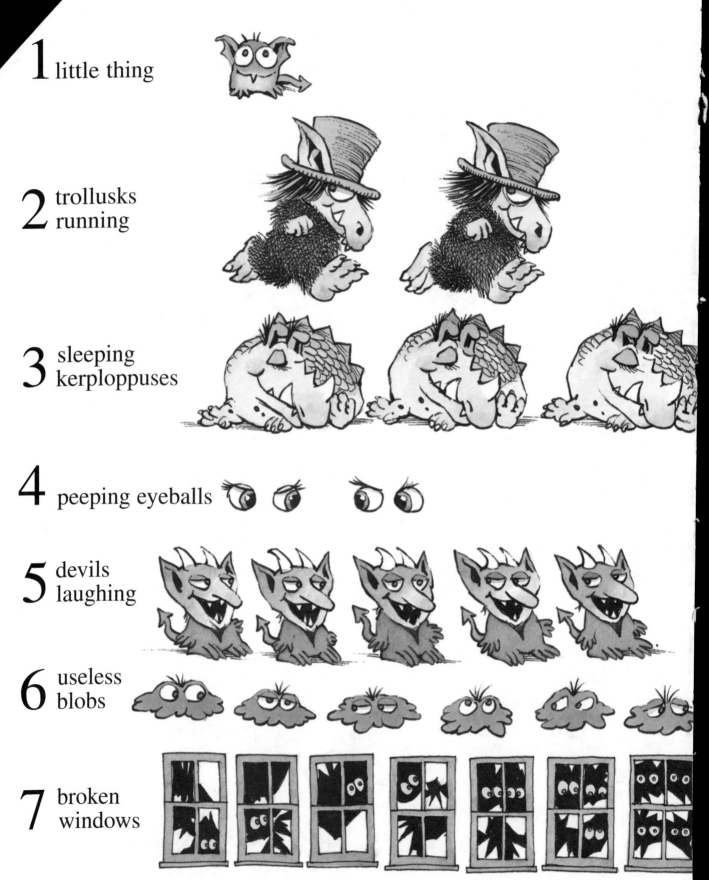

1 little thing

2 trollusks running

3 sleeping kerploppuses

4 peeping eyeballs

5 devils laughing

6 useless blobs

7 broken windows